Fly Fishing Basics 101

A Beginner's Guide to Equipment, Terminology, Flies and Casting Basics

Kurt Zeller

Copyright Act of 1976, the scanning, uploading and electronic sharing of any part of this book without the explicit written consent or permission of the publisher constitutes unlawful piracy and the theft of intellectual property.

If you would like to use material or content from this book (other than for review purposes), prior written permission must be obtained from the publisher.

You can contact the publishing company at admin@speedypublishing.com. Thank you for not infringing on the author's rights.

Speedy Publishing LLC (c) 2014
40 E. Main St., #1156
Newark, DE 19711
www.speedypublishing.co

Ordering Information:
Quantity sales; Special discounts are available on quantity purchases by corporations, associations, and others. For details, contact the "Special Sales Department" at the address above.

This is a reprint book.

Manufactured in the United States of America

TABLE OF CONTENTS

PUBLISHER'S NOTES i

CHAPTER 1: FLY FISHING INTRODUCTION 1

CHAPTER 2: FLY FISHING TERMINOLOGY 3

CHAPTER 3: FLY FISHING GEAR YOU NEED 15

CHAPTER 4: PUTTING THE REEL ON THE ROD 27

CHAPTER 5: THE MANY TYPES OF KNOTS 30

CHAPTER 6: FLY LINE CASTING BASICS 36

CHAPTER 7: TYING YOUR OWN FLIES 47

CHAPTER 8: LEARNING TO FIND WHERE THE FISH 56

CHAPTER 9: RECOMMENDED FLY FISHING LOCATIONS FOR YOUR BUCKET LIST
.... 60

CHAPTER 10: FLY FISHING ETIQUETTE 67

CHAPTER 11: CONCLUSION 71

MEET THE AUTHOR 73

Publisher's Notes

Disclaimer

This publication is intended to provide helpful and informative material. It is not intended to diagnose, treat, cure, or prevent any health problem or condition, nor is intended to replace the advice of a physician. No action should be taken solely on the contents of this book. Always consult your physician or qualified health-care professional on any matters regarding your health and before adopting any suggestions in this book or drawing inferences from it.

The author and publisher specifically disclaim all responsibility for any liability, loss or risk, personal or otherwise, which is incurred as a consequence, directly or indirectly, from the use or application of any contents of this book.

Any and all product names referenced within this book are the trademarks of their respective owners. None of these owners have sponsored, authorized, endorsed, or approved this book.

Always read all information provided by the manufacturers' product labels before using their products. The author and publisher are not responsible for claims made by manufacturers.

Chapter 1: Fly Fishing Introduction

It's a beautiful day in early spring. You are standing beside a beautiful river flowing through the mountains of Colorado. In your hands you hold your gear. You are brimming with excitement as you imagine what you will catch today. You are getting ready to fly fish and you can't wait to get started!

People have been fly fishing for years. In its beginnings, people would use flies to fish with for food, but then it turned into a sport and now anglers fly fish for both food and sport.

Fly fishing is a traditional angling method that uses artificial flies for lures that are made of materials like fur and feathers. The flies are fastened onto a hook and are meant to imitate a fish's natural food source. The rods are light, but the lines are heavy providing the weight and momentum for casting.

Fly fishermen use a series of casting moves meant to imitate the bug on water. The techniques are wide and varied. When casting much of the rod's movement comes from the angler's wrist.

Fly fishing as a sport is something many people find amazingly enjoyable. Most fly fishing is done in certain places like Colorado, Montana, and Wisconsin. The fish most often caught are trout and salmon, although anglers can catch a variety of fish with their flies.

In this book, we'll explore a variety of topics with regards to fly fishing. Some of the information will be geared towards beginning fishermen, but experienced fly fishers can benefit from this information as well. A refresher course is always good in any sport!

We'll look at the gear you'll need, ways to tie flies, and the best places to find an excellent fishing spot. You'll learn about places to buy your gear from and what to look for when you are buying that gear.

This author is an equal opportunity person and no disrespect is meant to women who like to fly fish when I use the term fisherman. Because most of the time we say the word "fisherman", don't fret gals, I'm talking about you too!

Let's explore the joys of fly fishing!

Chapter 2: Fly Fishing Terminology

Just as with any sport, there are some terms that are synonymous with the sport itself. While most people think of flies as pesky insects, fly fishermen know that flies are something else altogether. Flies to a fisherman are what is most important to make their hobby enjoyable and challenging.

To a beginner, fly fishing terminology might be confusing, so in this section, we'll present you with some new terms and what those terms mean so that when we use them later in this book, you'll know what we're talking about.

Back cast – The portion of any fly cast that extends beyond the person doing the casting.

Bass Bug - Name used to describe a large number of surface bass flies usually tied with hollow hair (such as deer hair).

Bass Bug Taper - A special weight forward floating fly line with a short front taper so that the generally wind-resistant bass bugs can turn over.

Blood Knot - The most widely used knot for tying two pieces of monofilament with similar diameters together; the best knot for construction of a knotted tapered leader; also called the barrel knot.

Breaking Strength - Amount of effort required to break a single strand of unknotted monofilament or braided line, usually stated in pounds (example: 6 lb. test).

Caddis - One of the three most important aquatic insects imitated by fly fishermen; found worldwide in all freshwater habitats; adult resembles a moth when in flight; at rest the wings are folded in a tent shape down the back; the most important aquatic state of the caddis is the pupa, which is its emerging stage.

Casting Arc - The path that the fly rod follows during a complete cast, usually related to the face of a clock.

Clinch Knot - Universally used knot for attaching a hook, lure, swivel, or fly to the leader or line; a slight variation results in the improved clinch knot, which is an even stronger knot for the above uses.

Co-Polymers – These are mixtures of various nylons and plastics along with anti-UV chemicals that have resulted in the exceptionally high breaking strength of modern tippet material. This is certainly one of the biggest advancements in fly fishing in the last 50 years. It allows you to use very fine tippets with breaking strengths two to four times as strong as regular nylon monofilament. Co-polymers are not as abrasion resistant as regular nylon monofilament.

Damping - Reducing excess vibrations in the rod blank when unloading the rod during a cast. This causes fewer waves in your fly line resulting in more power & distance for less effort.

Dead Drift - A perfect float meaning the fly is traveling at the same pace as the current; used in both dry fly and nymph fishing.

Double Taper (DT) - A standard fly line design in which both ends of the line are tapered, while the greater portion or "belly" of the line is level; excellent line for short to moderate length casts, and for roll casting; not as well suited for distance casts; commonly available in floating, or sinking styles.

Drag - (1) Term used to describe an unnatural motion of the fly caused by the effect of the current on line and leader. Drag is usually detrimental, though at times useful such as when imitating the actions of the adult caddis. (2) Resistance applied to the reel spool to prevent it from turning faster than the line leaving the spool which is used in playing larger fish.

Dry Fly - Any fly fished upon the surface of the water; usually constructed of non-water-absorbent materials; most commonly used to imitate the adult stage of aquatic insects.

Dry Fly Floatant – This is a chemical preparation that is applied to a dry fly before use to waterproof it; may be a paste, liquid, or aerosol.

False Cast - Standard fly fishing cast; used to lengthen and shorten line, to change direction, and to dry off the fly; frequently overused. In false casting, the line is kept moving backwards and forwards without being allowed to touch the surface of the water or the ground.

Floating Fly Line - a fly line where the entire line floats; best all round fly line.

Fly Casting - standard method of presenting a fly to a target using a fly rod and fly line; involves many different casts.

Fly Line - key ingredient to fly fishing; made of a tapered plastic coating over a braided Dacron or nylon core; available in several tapers and in floating, sinking, and sink-tip styles.

Fly Reel - fishing reel used in fly fishing to hold the fly line. There are three basic types: single action, multiplier, and automatic. 1.) Single action is the most common and the most popular. Single action means that one turn of the handle equals one turn of the spool. 2.) Multiplying reels use a gear system to increase this ratio (usually, 2-to-1). With a 2-to-1 ratio, each turn of the handle equals 2 revolutions of the spool. 3.) Automatic fly reels are the least practical for most people; they operate by a manually wound spring which is activated by a lever; automatic reels are heavy and tend to malfunction.

Fly Rod - a type of fishing rod especially designed to cast a fly line. Fly rods differ from other types of rods in that the reel attaches at the butt of the rod with the rod handle always above the reel; fly rods usually have more line guides than other types of rods of the same length. Fly rod lengths vary, with common lengths being between 7 and 9 feet. Materials used in fly rod construction are bamboo, fiberglass, and graphite.

Forceps - hand operated medical instrument widely used in fly-fishing to remove flies from the jaws of a hooked fish. Have pliers-like jaws with locking clips so that once they are clamped to the hook, they stay there until you release them.

Forward Cast - the front portion of the false cast or pick-up and lay-down, and a mirror image of the back cast.

Freestone – this is a type of river or stream with a significant gradient resulting in medium to fast-moving water. Although the upper reaches of a freestone stream may be spring-fed, the vast majority of its flow comes from run-off or tributaries. The fast moving water inhibits the growth of weeds or other rooted vegetation resulting in a "Free Stone" bottom. Freestone streams are less fertile than spring creeks resulting in a smaller and less diverse aquatic insect population. Fewer bugs in faster water usually results in fewer but more opportunistic trout.

Gel-spun polyethylene – This is a synthetic fiber that is extremely thin, supple, slippery, very abrasion resistant, and strong. It is stronger than steel for its size. It is often used as a braided fly line backing where large amounts of backing are needed and space on the reel is limited.

Graphite - the most popular rod-building material in use today; offers the best weight, strength, and flex ratio of any rod building material currently available.

Hackle - a feather, usually from the neck area of a chicken; can be any color (dyed or natural); hackle quality, such as the stiffness of the individual fibers and amount of web, determines the type of fly tied with the hackle; many hackles are grown specifically for fly tying.

Headwaters - upstream section of the river before the main tributaries join it. This section is typically much smaller in width and flow than the main section of the river.

Hollow Hair - hair from some animals is mostly hollow, thus holding air and making these hairs float. Hollow hair is ideal for tying dry flies and bass bugs. Antelope, deer, and elk all have hollow hair.

Hook – a hook is the object upon which the fly is tied; can be any size from tiny to huge; made from steel wire, and either bronzed, cadmium coated, or stainless. Hook designs are variable; style used depends upon the type of fly being tied.

Imitative Flies- flies tied to more closely match specific insects. Imitative flies are most effective in slow-moving, clear water, with finicky trout in fertile streams with large populations of aquatic insects.

Impressionistic Flies - flies tied to loosely suggest a variety of insects or insect families. For instance, a Hare's Ear nymph in sizes 12-16 can be used as both a mayfly and a caddis fly imitation and in larger sizes as a stonefly imitation. Impressionistic flies are usually most effective in medium to fast water, in streams with sparser populations of aquatic insects.

Indicator - floating object placed on the leader or end of the fly line to "indicate" the take of the fly by a fish or to indicate the path of the drift of the fly; used when nymph fishing with a slack line; very effective.

Knotless Tapered Leader - a fly fishing leader entirely constructed from a single piece of monofilament. Extrusion or acid immersion is most commonly used to taper the leader.

Knotted Leader – this is a fly fishing leader constructed by knotting sections of different diameter leader material to each other to make a tapered leader. Most commonly used knots to construct such a leader are blood (or barrel) knot and surgeon's knot.

Leader – the leader is the section of monofilament line between the fly line and the fly. It is usually tapered, so that it will deliver the fly softly and away from the fly line.

Leader Material – leader material is clear nylon or other type of monofilament. Two types are commonly used. One is the stiff or hard type, used mainly for the butt section and saltwater leaders; the second type is soft or supple monofilament, used mostly for tippets on all line weights, and for complete leaders on light weight fly lines.

Level Line - an un-tapered fly line, usually floating. It is difficult to cast, a poor line for delicacy or distance, and a poor choice for an all round line.

Loading the Rod - phrase used to describe the bend put in the rod by the weight of the line as it travels through the air during the cast.

Mayfly - worldwide, the most commonly imitated aquatic insect. Most dry fly and nymph patterns imitate this insect. Nymph stage of the mayfly lasts approximately one year; adult stages last one to three days. The adult has one pair of upright wings, making it look like a small sailboat. Mayflies are commonly found in cold or cool freshwater environments.

Mending Line - method used after the line is on the water to achieve a drag free float. It constitutes a flip, or series of flips with the rod tip, which puts a horseshoe shaped bow in the line. This slows down the speed with which the line travels if mended upstream, and speeds up the line if mended downstream. For example: if a cast is across the flow of the stream and the fastest part of the current is on your side, the mends would typically be made upstream to slow the line down so it keeps pace with the fly traveling in the slower current across from you.

Midge - a term properly applied to the small Dipterans that trout feed on. Many people call them gnats. Adult's appearance is similar to mosquitoes. Midges have two wings that lie in a flat "V" shape over the back when at rest. They are also known as "the fly fisher's curse" because of their small size and trout's affinity to feeding upon them. The term "midge" is sometimes loosely applied (and incorrectly so) when referring to small mayflies.

Monofilament - a clear, supple nylon filament used in all types of fishing that is available in many breaking strengths and diameters.

Nail Knot- method used to attach a leader or butt section of monofilament to the fly line, and of attaching the backing to the fly line; most commonly tied using a small diameter tube rather than a nail.

Narrow Loop - term that describes what the fly line should look like as it travels through the air; a narrow loop can best be described as the letter "U" turned on its side; it is formed by using a narrow casting arc.

Needle Nail Knot - same as the nail knot except that the leader or backing is run up through the center of the fly line for 3/16 to 3/8 inch, then out through the side of the fly line before the nail knot is tied; this allows the backing or the leader to come out the center of the fly line rather than along the side of it as in the nail knot.

Nymph - immature form of insects; as fly fishers, we are concerned only with the nymphs of aquatic insects.

Nymphing - word describing fish feeding on nymphs; nymphing right at the surface can be difficult to tell from fish feeding on adults, careful observation should tell.

Open Loop - term used to describe what the fly line looks like as it travels through the air during a poor cast; caused by a very wide casting arc.

Pick-up & Lay Down - a fly fishing cast using only a single back cast. The line is lifted from the water and a back cast made, followed by a forward cast which is allowed to straighten and fall to the water, completing the cast; good wet fly cast; also useful in bass bugging; most efficient cast to use, when possible, because the fly spends more time in the water (also see presentation).

Popping Bug a bass bug made from a hard material. Usually cork or balsa woods, as these are high floating materials that can be made into a variety of shapes.

Presentation - the act of putting the fly on the water and offering it to the fish; the variety of presentations is infinite, and changes with each fishing situation. The object is to present the fly in a manner similar to the natural insect or food form that you are imitating.

Reel Seat - mechanism that holds the reel to the rod, usually using locking metal rings or sliding bands.

Retrieve - bringing the fly back towards the caster after the cast is made; can be done in a variety of ways; important points of retrieving are to keep the rod tip low and pointed straight down the line.

Rod Flex - The manner in which the rod bends during the cast during the acceleration phase of the cast. Tip-Flex rods bend primarily through the tip section, Mid-Flex rods bend down into the middle section, and Full-flex rods bend throughout the entire rod during the cast.

Roll Cast - one of the three most basic fly casts; allows a cast to be made without a back cast; essential for use with sinking lines, to bring the line to the surface so it may be picked up and cast in a normal manner.

Running Line - a thin line attached to the back of a shooting taper (shooting head) line. The line may be 20 to 30 pound monofilament, braided nylon, narrow floating or sinking line, or other material. Usually 100 feet in length, it allows the fly fisher to quickly change the type of line being used by interchanging only the head section.

"S" Cast - cast used to put deliberate and controlled slack into a cast; used in getting a drag free float and in conjunction with mending line.

Saltwater Taper - a weight forward fly line that is similar to a bass bug taper.

Setting the Hook – this is the act of pulling the hook into the flesh of the fish's mouth. The amount of effort needed to do this varies with the size of hook, type of fish, and breaking strength of leader; most people strike too hard on trout and warm water fish and not hard enough on salmon and saltwater fish.

Shooting Taper or Shooting Head - a short single tapered fly line, 30-38 feet long; shooting heads are designed for longest casts with minimum effort; shooting heads allow quick change of line types (floating, sinking, sink-tip, etc.) by quickly interchanging head sections; shooting heads are most commonly used with salmon, steelhead, saltwater, and shad fishing, though they can be used in all types of fly fishing.

Sink Rate - the speed at which a sinking fly line sinks; there are at least 6 different sink rates for fly lines, from very slow to extremely fast.

Sink-Tip Fly Line - a floating fly line where the tip portion sinks; available in 4 foot, 10 foot, 12 foot, 15 foot, 20 foot, 24 foot, and 30 foot sinking tips; the 10 foot sink-tips are most commonly used and are practical in many applications; sink-tip lines are useful in all types of fly fishing, but especially in wet fly or streamer fishing.

Sinking Fly Line – this is a fly line in which the entire length of the line sinks beneath the surface of the water.

Spool – the spool is the part of the fly reel that revolves and which holds the backing and the fly line; may be purchased separately.

Standing Line - the part of the line that is joined to another piece of line when tying the tag ends together. Two standing lines are joined by tying their tag ends into a knot.

Stonefly - very important aquatic insect; nymph lives for one to three years, depending on species; most species hatch out by crawling to the shoreline and emerging from its nymphal case above the surface, thus adults are available to trout only along shoreline and around midstream obstructions; adult has two pair of wings which are folded flat along its back when at rest; stoneflies require a rocky bottomed stream with very good water quality.

Streamer - fly tied to imitate the various species of baitfish upon which game fish feed; usually tied using feathers for the wing, but can be tied with hair and/or feathers; tied in all sizes.

Stripping line - Retrieving the line by pulling it in through your fingers as opposed to winding it in on the reel. Term sometimes used to refer to running line (not a common usage).

Surgeon's Knot - excellent knot used to tie two lengths of monofilament together; the lines may be of dissimilar diameters.

Tag (Tag End) - the end of the line that is used to tie a knot.

Tapered Leader - a leader made of monofilament and used for fly fishing; the back or butt section of the leader is of a diameter nearly as large as the fly line, then becomes progressively smaller in diameter as you approach the tip end.

Tippet - the end section of a tapered leader; the smallest diameter section of a tapered leader; the fly is tied onto the tippet.

Turn Over - words that describe how the fly line and leader straighten out at the completion of the cast.

Unloading the Rod - unbending the rod or transferring the casting energy from the rod back into the fly line.

Waders - high topped waterproof boots; two main types used in fishing: boot foot and stocking foot; boot foot have boots built in, just pull on and go; stocking foot requires the use of a pair of wading shoes and provides better support and traction.

Wading Shoes - shoes built specifically to be worn over stocking foot waders; can be made of leather, nylon or other synthetic materials.

Weight Forward - an easy casting fly line because it carries most of its weight in the forward section of the line; instead of a level middle section, like a double taper, it quickly tapers down to a fine diameter running line which shoots through the guides with less resistance for added distance; the most versatile fly line.

Wet Fly - (1) any fly fished below the surface of the water; nymphs and streamers are wet flies (2) a traditional style of fly tied with soft, swept back hackle, and a backward sweeping wing; the forerunner of the nymph and streamer.

Wet Fly Swing – this is the typical presentation method for fishing a wet fly. Cast the fly downstream and across, and then swim it across the current. A wet fly swing is commonly used to imitate swimming mayflies, emerging caddis, and small fish.

Wind Knot - an overhand knot put in the leader by poor casting, greatly reducing the breaking strength of the leader.

As you read through this book, refer to this glossary if you don't understand what a term means. We have tried to provide a comprehensive list of the most commonly used terms that you may come across.

You will need to have the right equipment if you are going to be fly fishing as a hobby or as a sport. There are just certain things you can't do without.

Chapter 3: Fly Fishing Gear You Need

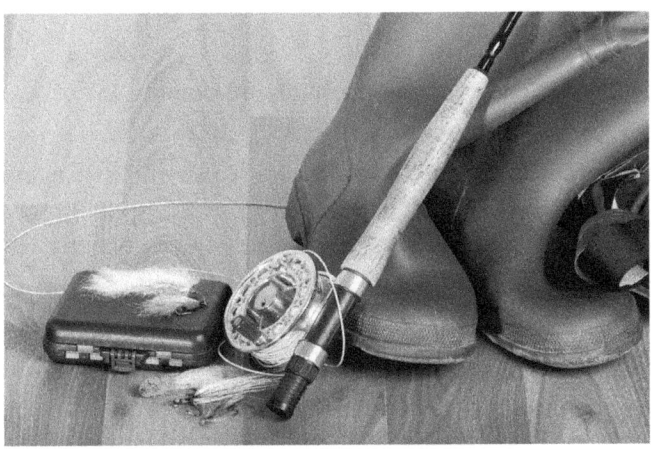

Fly fishing isn't the cheapest sport in the world when it comes to getting outfitted with all the gear you need. But the truth of the matter is that when you invest in some quality equipment, you'll not only enjoy the sport more, but you'll have better luck catching the fish you dreamed of when you have the right equipment.

Let's start with clothing. You can wear anything you want underneath the vest and waders, but these two items of apparel are vital to successful fly fishing.

Vests

Fly fishing requires a lot of parts and accessories. You'll have to carry them all with you, and the most efficient way to do this is with a fishing vest. These vests have many, many pockets where you can stow all your gear like flies, lines, weights, etc. Here are some things to consider when buying your fly fishing vest:

- What types of weather conditions will you be encountering during your fly fishing trips? Weather and temperature are both huge considerations when it comes to your fishing vest. If you will be fishing mostly in warm weather, get a mesh vest that is more ventilated. For colder weather, get a vest that is big enough to allow for layers underneath so that you don't freeze!

- When fly fishing, you will probably be doing a lot of wading in water, so you will want a vest with a short waist. This will keep your equipment above the waterline and avoid damaging it.

- Think seriously about how much you will be carrying with you. Lots of pockets are great, but if you fill all of them up with unnecessary equipment, you'll weigh yourself down. You will, however, want a vest with various sizes of pockets to accommodate the different things you will be carrying with you.

- The pockets in your vest should be easy to open and close. Ideally, you should be able to get in them with just one hand. Vests with Velcro to seal them are the best, and look for one with a "D-ring" on the back so you have someplace to hold your net.

- Make sure that you can move easily once your vest is filled with your chosen equipment. If you are weighed down too much, casting can become difficult.

- Vests come in various colors, and you will want to pick one that blends with the vegetation of the area you will be fishing. Tan is good for fishing in the West and green will match the foliage of the East.

- Also find a vest with few places where your line can get caught during casting. Lines and leaders have a nasty habit of getting caught on fly patches, zippers, sunglass holders, and anything else that sticks out on your vest.

Just find a vest within your budget that meets the basic guidelines listed above and you should be ready to go.

Waders

Waders are a combination of pants and boots all in one piece that will keep you dry inside while you're wading in the water. That's why they call them waders! The last thing you want is to have your waders leaking while you are waist deep in a cold Colorado River in November. What do you look for in a good pair of waders? Here are a few suggestions:

- Waders can be used for a variety of outdoor activities like duck hunting, goose hunting, and, of course, fishing. Consider what your primary use of your waders is going to be. If you fish more than you hunt, then the type, thickness, and color of your waders is going to be important. Consider what the temperature of the water is going to be when you wear your waders. That will determine how thick your waders need to be.

- The material of your waders can be very important as well. Again, you will need to take into consideration what type of weather condition you be wearing them in. Here are some of the more popular materials:

  ❖ Neoprene – This is the most popular material for waders. It is very durable and can take a lot of abuse. It comes in many thicknesses, so you can choose the one that will best fit your needs: 3mm or 5mm. 3mm is best for places where it is usually of moderate weather with a few cold days. This is also a good thickness if you have to walk a ways to get to your fishing spot or if you walk a lot while you're fishing. 5mm is the choice for colder weather spots or if you want to use your waders for hunting as well.

- ❖ Gore Tex – This type of material is relatively new and is a breathable fabric that is comfortable and watertight. It allows moisture to escape even while in the water. These types of waders can be worn in the summer time and sweat is not an issue. They can also be worn in the winter with a pair of sweat pants underneath and the moisture will be released keeping you dry. These types of waders are also very comfortable and are conducive to walking while fishing.

- ❖ Canvas – These are considered "old school" waders and are hard to find anymore. While they are durable and cheaper than other materials, you will sacrifice comfort, flexibility, and breathability when you choose canvas as a material.

- ❖ Nylon – Lightweight and will keep you dry and warm. However, nylon waders can get quite warm inside because they are not made of a breathable material and when you sweat inside them, you could get quite uncomfortable. Because of the accumulation of moisture, this could lead to hypothermia in cold weather.

- ❖ Rubber – This material was long considered the one of choice among fishermen because the rubber waders are generally cheaper. But the drop in price for neoprene and Gore Tex has caused rubber waders to drop in popularity. You will have less flexibility and virtually no breathability with rubber waders, plus they can be cumbersome.

- Getting your waders to fit right is also very important. If your waders don't fit right, you will find yourself tiring more easily and growing uncomfortable just a short time into your fishing expedition. Your waders should provide enough room so that you can wear clothing underneath without being too tight. If you order your waders off the Internet, make sure the site has your height, weight, and shoe size. They should be able to guide you toward the right pair. If you go to a sporting goods store, take the time to try on the waders. Do a couple of knee bends and walk around. Put your foot up on a chair and make sure that they don't ride up on you.

- You will also need to make a decision as to what type of boot and boot soles to get. Some waders have the boots connected to the wader in one piece. If you are going to spend most of your fishing and hunting time in cold weather, this type of wader should be your first choice. They provide the best cold water protection and most are insulated. This type of wader is also very easy to put on and take off. Stocking foot waders are quite popular these days among hunters and fishers. This is because of their weight advantage. They are constructed the same way as boot waders but without the built-in boots. This type of wader has a neoprene sock attached, so you will have to get a separate pair of wading boots. Be aware that if you pick stocking waders, the possibility of gravel and debris getting into your boots is greater and can cause great discomfort for you.

Chest high waders are the best kind to get so that you can go into deeper water without getting wet. When you get your waders home, they should be washed off thoroughly. Wash your wading boots as well. It's also a good idea to wash the waders down with a 10 percent bleach solution after you've been fishing to kill any possible molds or fish diseases that might be clinging to the material.

Fly Rods

Fly rods and line weights are typically written as "Nwt" where the N is a number. For example, you can have 8wt, 9wt, etc. All rods are matched to fly lines according to weight. So if you have an 8wt rod, you'll need an 8wt fly line although you can safely go one number above or below the weight if need be.

It is important to use the correct fly line with the appropriate rod weight or it will significantly affect your casting performance. It can also warp the rod.

Some rods are multi-rated (7-8wt, 7-8-9wt, etc.). The advantage to a rod like this is that you have a variety of fly lines that you can use with the same rod. The disadvantage is that you will be sacrificing flexibility in the rod itself.

Selecting a fly rod depends a lot on what type of fish you will want to catch. Some rods are better suited for smaller fish and bigger fish. Here is an idea of the weight of rod you will need for certain situations:

- 1-3 Weight: delicate presentations with small flies, designed for trout or pan fish on small to moderate size waters

- 4-6 Weight: trout, pan fish, and small bass, 4wt is for delicate presentation, 5wt is good for trout on spring-fed creeks or bigger rivers, 6wt is best on big waters or in windy conditions

- 7-8 Weight: give extra power to land smallmouth bass, steelhead, and bigger trout in rivers or reservoirs; work best with bigger flies; good for steelhead, redfish, snook, or light salmon fishing

- 9-10 Weight: good for larger flies and catching salmon and pike; also work good in saltwater with medium-sized fish

- 11 Weight and Up: this is for the larger fish like tarpon, tuna, billfish

There are basically two types of materials that rods can be made of: fiberglass and graphite. There are advantages to either type of material.

Fiberglass rods are durable and generally less expensive. This is the most common type of material fly rods are made of. Fiberglass rods are a good choice for beginners because they can be used for a variety of fishing situations.

Graphite or composition rods are lighter and better at casting. These rods can also handle many type of fishing situations, so it's also a good choice for beginners as well as experienced fishermen. Graphite, however, will give you more fighting weight with your rod when it comes to landing your fish.

You can also use a bamboo rod which is what the earliest fly fishing rods were made of. Bamboo rods can be quite expensive. These rods offer grace, form, and strength. They demand a slow or soft casting style that is suited to slow, leisurely fishing. Beginners should shy away from bamboo rods because they can be a bit difficult to control in certain situations.

Rod lengths can have an effect on casting action. In general, longer rods give more action while shorter rods are geared for tighter situations such as narrow streams. Consider the following guidelines:

- Less than 8 foot: These are short rods and are good for fishing tight areas such as narrow streams with overhanging trees or small ponds with lots of brush.

- 8 – 9 feet: These lengths are good for trout and bass fishing. The longer length will give more casting range and improve line control.

- 9 feet and longer: This length is designed for long casts and better ability to manage line. This size rod is good for open waters and fishing from float tubes.

If you are a beginner, it's a good idea to start with a pre-packaged combo. These types of rods will give you a better chance of landing a fish and lead to your enjoyment of the sport. Look for a 5-6 weight rod and reel in an 8 or 9 foot length. This type of combo will allow you to fish in all sorts of situations.

Fly Reels

Just like when picking out your wader and rod, when choosing a reel, you'll need to consider what type of fish you will be fishing for. You can't catch a big game fish like a tarpon with a small reel or you're setting yourself up for some big trouble.

At one point in time, fly reels were thought of as just storage devices. In use, a fly fishermen strips line off the reel with one hand, casting the rod with the other, and then retrieving slack line by rotating the reel spool.

Manually-operated fly reels have traditionally been rather simple in terms of mechanical construction, with a simple click-pawl drag system. However, in recent years, more advanced fly reels have been developed for larger fish and more demanding conditions.

Newer reels often feature disc-type drags to permit the use of lighter leaders and tippets, or to successfully capture fish that pull long lengths of line/leader. Many newer fly reels have large-arbor designs to increase speed of retrieve and improve drag performance during long runs. In order to prevent corrosion, saltwater fly reels often use aerospace aluminum frames and spools, stainless steel components and sealed bearing/drive mechanisms.

Fly reels are generally made of aluminum. Some cheap reels are made of castings while the more expensive ones are bar stock that is hand turned on lathes. Pressed reels, while cheaper, don't have the strength that bar stock reels have.

A reel is connected to the seat with a long sanded metal object called the reel feet. The feet slide into bands or clips called a reel seat. All reels are made on one standard so seats on rods will accept any reel.

A reel has a handle of course which is used to turn the spool. There are several creative designs but most are screwed into the spool, some are machined and attached to the face. Usually in fly tackle we have only one handle, although some designs have two knobs. A handle should be secure, not wiggle and be solidly attached. I have seen a few that barely get the job done. Some have knobs that spin freely, while the handle itself is stationary. Most are metal although some have wood or plastic inserts.

A spool is the part of the reel that holds the line. Attached to the outside of the spool is a small weight that is called a counter balance. This acts as balance so that the spool spins freely and true. In most modern reels, the counter balance is decoration but in older reels, if the weight wasn't there it didn't turn true. This is primarily due to the weight and size of the reel. Think of the counter balance like the weights on your tires.

Spools generally have exposed rims; this is called the palming rim. If you are playing a fish you can cup your hand on the outside of the rim and slow the fish or play it with a palming rim. If you are playing a fish on light tackle with light tippets, this often is a better choice because it doesn't stress the tip of your rod as much or risk breaking the tip of the rod. It also can help you from breaking off the fish when using light tippets.

The arbor is the center of the reel. A large arbor has a large inside center while a regular arbor has a smaller inside center post. Usually large arbor reels are heavier while a small arbor reel is lighter. The main advantage here is that a large arbor makes the line pick up faster and creates fewer coils in the line.

If you don't use a lot of backing when spooling the line, you will pack it in tightly creating lots of coils. When you cast this out, it will cork screw and spin almost any fly into a doughnut. This is one reason for using backing or also to increase the size of the reel as you up the size of the line. If you have a small arbor with little backing, don't leave the reel in hot trunk of your car or you are likely to make permanent sets and coils into the line.

Drags are the part of the reel that creates pressure and prevents the line from free spooling or back lashing. The drag is created in several ways: spring /pawl or disc drag. Click drags are springs that mostly put pressure against a gear and keep it from free spooling. It doesn't create a lot of pressure on the line and mostly is an anti-back lash thing. These reels are noisy.

Disc drags are either pads or gears. In a pad system the drag has a caliper like the breaks on a car, the caliper clamps against a disc and as the pressure increases, the clamp tightens. A gear system uses bearings and gears and a one way clip that controls the amount of pressure against the gears. As the pressure increases, the force increases.

Again, you need to consider what type of fishing you will be doing when choosing your reel. The larger the fish, the larger the reel you will need.

Fly Lines

Fly lines come in a variety of forms. They may have varying diameters or tapered section or a level (even) diameter. A fly line may float, sink, or have a floating main section with a sinking tip.

A fly line consists of a tough braided or monofilament core wrapped in a thick waterproof plastic sheath often made of polyvinyl chloride (PVC). In the case of floating fly lines, the PVC sheath is usually embedded with many "micro-balloons" or air bubbles and may also contain silicone or other lubricants to give buoyancy and reduce wear.

Fly lines also come in a variety of models for use in specific environments. These climates include fresh water, salt water, cold, or tropical temperatures, etc.

All fly lines are matched to the individual rod according to weight. Because the fly line and not the lure determine casting, fly rods are sized according to the size of fly line and not the weight of the lure. Fly lines comes in a wide range of numbered sizes from a small #0 to a strong #16. They also come in many profiles such as double-tapered, weight-forward, shooting-head, etc.

Most fly lines are only around 90 feet long which is sufficient for sporting purposes. Specialized shooting-head lines with a short, heavy front section and small-diameter backing are often used for long-distance casting as well as competitive events.

To fill up the reel spool and insure an adequate reserve in case of a run by a powerful fish, fly lines are usually attached to a secondary line at the butt section which is called backing. Fly line backing is usually composed of braided Dacron or Gelspun monofilaments. Backing varies in length according to the type of fish. Seventy-five yards is used for smaller freshwater species and as much as 400 yards is for large saltwater game fish.

All fly lines are equipped with a leader of monofilament or fluorocarbon fishing line usually tapered in diameter and referred to by the "X-size" (0X, 2X, etc.) of its final tip section or tippet. For example, a freshwater trout leader might have a butt section of 20 point test monofilament tapering through 15, 12, 10, and 8-pound test sections and terminating in a 5X tippet. A fly line is only as strong as its weakest link which is the final tippet section.

Where can you find your equipment? Many places carry fly fishing equipment. Local sporting goods stores are a good place to start. You may want to look on the Internet for a place like Cabela's or Bass Pro Shops. Orvis is another good place to find your fly fishing equipment.

Some towns and cities have specialty fishing stores as well. These can be extremely helpful places to go as they will have all the latest information on where to fish, what to look for in certain pieces of equipment, and recommendations on what types of equipment would work best for you.

Now that you have all of this equipment, what do you do next?

Chapter 4: Putting the Reel on the Rod

Before you start putting together your rod take some paraffin wax and rub in on the male parts of the rod where it goes together. Don't be afraid of using too much. You can always rub it off later. This will keep the sections from coming loose and it will also keep it from sticking together.

Next, put the reel on. The reel fits into the reel-seat, one 'foot' of the reel slides into a slot in the reel seat. The reel is secured to the rod with the sliding or screw rings. There are both 'up-locking' and 'down-locking' reel seats.

Which way to use the reel? Most prefer for a right hander to have the handles on the left side. If you will cast with your right hand, keep the rod in that hand and reel with your left. At least start out that way. You can always change later if you want to.

Check to make sure your reel is set-up for left hand retrieve by pulling out some line and noticing if the drag engages going out or coming in. It should be 'on' when the line is going out. Most reels are convertible to right or left hand retrieve. There should be instructions for changing it with the reel.

Now as you put the rod together, start with the eyes misaligned and 'twist' the sections together. Don't make it a straight pull; twist them about ninety degrees or so. When you are done make sure they are all nicely in line. This will seat them properly. Check the sections often to make sure they still have some paraffin; it can wear off over a season.

Presuming you already have the line on the reel, put the butt of the rod on the ground and after folding a small loop in the fly line, start poking it up through the guides. Don't put the line through the tiny little loop right by the cork, that's a hook keeper.

As the rod is a few feet taller than you are you could have a problem here. You can try jumping at the top guides but this has always proven a poor method. Try this. With the butt section on the ground, and the reel on YOUR side, angle the rod to your left and easily walk to your left as you continue stringing it. This will also make others think you just may know something about how to string a fly rod.

With your right hand, hold onto the tip of the rod. With your left hand carefully pull out the fly line, pull out about ten feet of fly line and the leader too. Be careful. This is a critical time. Many rods are broken by not doing it this way. Now your rig is together.

Pick up the rod and pull line straight off of the reel. That means 'straight' off, pulling toward the stripping guide, not down and against the edge of the reel. That will damage the fly line. You are now ready to cast.

If your reel was not filled when you got it, here are a few pointers. Backing (a bit like kite string) is used to help fill the reel so the fly line is near the top of the reel. This makes for larger coils of line which are better than little kinky ones. Fasten the backing to the reel with the 'Arbor knot'.

You can use a 'Nail Knot' to tie the fat end of the leader to the end of the fly line, for small rods and small fish. A better method is to put a 'Perfection Loop' in the fat end of the leader and use another knot of your choice to connect them. A 'blood knot' is often used to tie on a section of 'tippet material' to the leader if desired. Last, with a clinch knot, is the fly.

This seems like a great time to go ahead and address the different types of knots that are helpful to know.

Chapter 5: The Many Types of Knots

There are many different knots that you can use to tie your fly lines. Any one of them will work just fine. Which one you choose is a matter of personal preference. It is important that you tie the knot correctly and secure it properly. Failing to do so will result in lost fish and a lot of frustration.

Before you tighten a knot, you should wet it either with saliva or by dipping it in water. This will help the knot slide and seat properly. Lubrication also decreases excessive heat which dramatically weakens monofilament. Heat is generated by the friction created when knots are drawn up tight.

Seating the knot means to tie it tightly. Tighten knots with a steady, continuous pull. Make sure the knot is tight and secure. After it is tied, pull on the line and leader to make sure it holds. It is better to test it now than when a fish is on.

You will also need to trim the ends neatly. Use nippers to trim the material as close as possible without nicking or damaging the knot.

Here are a few of the more common knots you can try:

Albright

The Albright knot is used in situations where you need to join two lines of greatly unequal diameter or of different material. Mostly used in saltwater situations, you can also use this knot for joining of fly line to backing material.

Step 1: Loop the heavier line (wider diameter) and place it between your thumb and index finger of your left hand. Pass the lighter line through the formed loop leaving about 8 inches. Pinch the lighter line in with the line already in your left hand. (See illustration 1)

Step 2: Make approximately 10 wraps with the lighter line wrapping away from you and working from left to right. With each wrap, work your thumb and index finger along holding these wraps in place, trying not to let up any pressure on your left hand. On the 10th wrap, come around and then through the remaining loop.

Take the standing line in your right hand and pull gently as you push the wraps with your left hand towards the closed loop. Alternate between the end of the lighter line and on the standing part until the wraps are against the tag end. Make sure the wraps do not go over each other and that you don't push them too far. Pull the tag tight then pull on the standing part of both lines until the knot is secure.

Step 3: Finally, clip the two short pieces close to the knot.

Arbor Knot (Backing To Reel)

Step 1: Wrap the line around the arbor of your spool and tie an overhand knot around the standing line.

Step 2: Tie a second overhand knot on the tag end a few inches from the first.

Step 3: Moisten the line and the two overhand knots. Tighten the smaller knot and holding the spool in your left-hand pull on the standing line with your right hand sliding the first overhand knot against the arbor of the spool. The second overhand knot will keep this from slipping. Trim the tag end.

Blood Knot (Monofilament to Monofilament)

The blood knot is a knot used for attaching two pieces of monofilament together, primarily for rebuilding tapered leaders. This is an extremely strong knot when formed properly and should be tied with monofilament close in diameter. Best use is for monofilament 10 lbs. and up.

Step 1: Lay both sections of monofilament across one another. Wrap one section 5-6 times around the other bringing the end back down through the loop formed by both. (See illustration 1)

Step 2: Wrap the other line 5-6 times around the remaining portion of the first line and pass it's free end up through the formed loop. (See illustration 2)

Step 3: Moisten the knot with your mouth, and while holding the long ends pull the knot tight. Clip the short ends close and the knot is complete.

Turle Knot

The Turle knot is ideal when tying on flies with turned-up or turned-down eyes to your leader. This gives your fly good action because of the way the knot causes the leader to pull away from the hook. It can be tied with one or two wraps of an overhand knot.

Step 1: Pass the leader end through the hook-eye. Take two wraps around the standing line and pass the tag end through the loops forming a simple overhand knot. Tighten it down.

Step 2: Pass the fly through the large loop formed and snug it against the hook-eye.

Step 3: Tighten down and trim off the excess.

Improved Clinch Knot (Leader to Fly)

The Improved Clinch knot is used for fastening the leader to the fly. If you are using over 12 Lb. test line, this is not a recommended knot.

Step 1: Thread your leader tippet through the eye of the hook. Wrap the end of the leader around the standing line 5 times for lines up to 8lb test and 4 times for lines from 8-12lb test. (You can also turn the hook 5 or 4 times)

Step 2: Take the tag end of the leader and pass it through the gap between the eye of the hook and the first wrap. Continue the tag end back up through the main loop just formed.

Step 3: Moisten the knot with your mouth, and while holding the hook in your left-hand pull on the standing leader allowing the knot to seat tightly against the hook. Clip the excess line.

Non-Slip Mono Knot

The Non-Slip Mono Knot is extremely strong and as the name says, does mot slip like some of the other loop knots. This knot has been tested to close to 100% of the line strength. It is very important that you follow the wrap counts for maximizing its strength. 8X to 6lb test: 7 wraps. 8 to 12lbs: 5 wraps. 15lb to 40lb test: 4 wraps. 50-60lb test: 3 wraps, and up to 120lb test: 2 wraps.

Step 1: Take your line and form an over-hand knot, leaving approximately 8 inches. Pass the tag end through the eye of the hook. Bring the line back through the overhand knot the same side it came out. Make your wraps based upon the numbers above.

Step 2: After all the wraps are completed pass the line back through the over hand knot the same way it came out in the last step.

Step 3: Moisten the knot with your mouth, and while holding the hook in your right-hand pull slowly. As the knot tightens, take the standing line in your left hand and pull your hands apart finishing the knot. Finally, trim the ends.

Perfection Loop

The perfection loop knot is used for attaching two looped pieces of monofilament together. Sometimes used for a quick change of leaders. This is a dependable and strong when formed properly.

Step 1: Take the standing line in your left hand and form a loop by crossing the tag end over itself with your right hand. Pinch between the thumb and index finger in your left hand where it crosses leaving about 5 inches of the tag end exposed to work with. Form a smaller loop in front of the larger loop by bringing the tag end in front of the first formed loop. Pinch this in with the first crossover.

Step 2: Take the tag end, wrapping it around the back of both loops and then between the two loops. After you go between both loops add that to what you are pinching down between your fingers.

Step 3: With your right hand, reach through the first formed loop taking the second smaller loop between your thumb and index finger and pulls it through the first loop. Moisten and slowly pull on the standing line continuing to hold the smaller loop that you pulled through. Trim the tag end close and the loop knot is complete.

Surgeon's Knot

The Surgeon's Knot is a knot also used for attaching two pieces of monofilament together. It is a very fast and easy knot to tie and is usually preferred more than the blood knot. This is a great knot for joining two pieces of monofilament that are greatly different in diameter. When you are building a tapered leader, tied correctly, this knot is generally stronger than the blood knot. This is a very quick and easy knot for attaching 4X-5X-6X-7X tippet to each other. You can do this one in the dark.

Step 1: The main line should come in from the left and the line to be attached should come from the right. Overlap the two pieces approximately 6 or so inches. (See illustration 1)

Step 2: Pinch the overlapped lines together on the left between your thumb and index finger. Do the same with the sections on the right and make a loop by crossing it over itself. Take the long and short lines that are in your right hand and pass them through the formed loop, around, and back through a second time. (See illustration 2)

Step 3: Pull both pieces being held in each hand away from each other closing the knot. Moisten and pull tight. Once this not is secure you can tighten it further by pulling individual pieces. I would not recommend this knot for line over 30lbs because it will be hard to tighten and the strength of the knot will only be there if tightened all the way.

These are only a few of the knots you can use to tie your fly line. Ask others what they prefer and learn from your fishing buddies if you want. There are all sorts of knots and no one is better than another. As we've said, it's a matter of personal preference!

Since the basic idea in fly fishing is casting, let's look at a few casting techniques you can employ on your next excursion.

Chapter 6: Fly Line Casting Basics

You don't necessarily have to be a pro to know how to cast your fly line. Many people who are inept at casting can catch a myriad of fish, but once you know the basic rules for fly casting, you'll be well on your way to angling like the pros.

You'll need to start with the line straight and organized. You cannot move a fly with a slack line. If the line isn't straightened, you will waste time and energy on ineffective casts and you will place your rod in the wrong place. Always start tight. If the fly moves when the tip is moved just a little, the line is properly organized.

Every casting stroke is a smooth acceleration followed by a stop. Acceleration means that the rod pulls the line all through the cast. The cast is complete when the rod stops. The acceleration bends the rod and loads it like a spring. During acceleration, the rod bend increases, when it stops, the rod straightens propelling the line to where you want it to go.

Many experts liken this to flicking paint off of a paintbrush. Most people can understand this concept making it easier to learn a basic cast. The better the stop is, the more effective the cast is because the energy transfer from the rod to line is more efficient.

The line will always follow the rod tip. When the rod stops, the line will go in the direction the rod tip was going in when the stop was made. Thus, if you want your line to go straight, make your rod tip go straight.

There are two basic stances you can use when preparing to cast. The orthodox stance calls for you to put your foot below your casting arm shoulder and slightly in front of the other foot. For example, if you are casting with your right hand, the right foot should be slightly in front of the left foot. Your feet should be slightly apart, your body relaxed and comfortable. You should be able to transfer body weight easily between the feet during the cast.

If you use an open stance, your feet will be placed the opposite way of the orthodox stance. If you cast with your right hand, your right foot will be placed slightly behind the left foot. This type of position is used mainly for distance casting allowing the caster to turn and watch the back casting without moving or turning the shoulder.

When holding the rod, you should not hold on too tightly. If you grip the rod too tightly, you won't have smooth casts and it will cause muscle pain and fatigue in your arms with too tight of a grip.

The generally recommended way to hold your fly rod is to hold with the thumb on top and slightly to the left of center so that the "V" in between the thumb and index finger is in line with the top of the rod. As we've said, your grip must be comfortable and the size of the handle should fit nicely in your hand.

You can also choose to hold the rod with your index finger running on the top of the rod or slightly curled around and the handle resting comfortably in your palm. This grip is good for short distance accuracy.

Find which stance and which hold is right for you. The more you practice and play around with various holds and castings, the better you will get.

Overhead Cast

This is the most common type of cast used by fly fishermen. Start with the line straight out in front and straight to the rod top. Keep the tip low and avoid any slack in the line. Aim the rod slightly above straight out in front of you. The wrist, rod, hand, and lower arm should all move in unison. Accelerate the rod vertically until you are at approximately twelve o'clock at which time, the wrist breaks crisply driving the rod forward to about ten o'clock.

Overall, the arc may be slightly more than 90 degrees from start to finish. Movement starts slowly and then the speed of the rod tip increases rapidly toward the end of the stroke. Maximum input speed is reached immediately before the stop but the maximum delivery speed is after the stop.

If you do it correctly, the line will be flying upwards and behind you through the air and it will become fully straight. There will be no line tension in the rod. Arm and wrist positions remain stationary while the line is extending down the back cast.

When the line is fully extended behind, you should be able to feel the line loading in the rod tip by both the hand holding the rod and the other hand holding the line. During the forward cast, the wrist retains the "broken" position until the wrist straightens around eleven o'clock to give the line added push. The motion is checked crisply at ten o'clock allowing the line to extend straight with a well-formed loop uncoiling directly above the line from the rod tip.

You can remember the overhead cast by keeping in mind the following:

- TIP – tip of the rod down
- TOP – to the top and then pause
- TEN – stop at ten o'clock and stop and drop to keep the line straight as it falls

To practice, try standing with your arm straight down. Bend your elbow horizontal with your index finger pointing straight ahead. That is the starting position for the cast. Move your hand upward until your index finger touches the top of your ear. This is the position for completion of the back cast portion. If you look out of the corner of your eye, you should be able to see the inside of your palm.

To simulate the forward cast, let your hand fall to the ten o'clock position which will be just below shoulder height. Then you will have completed all three stopping positions for a basic overhead cast. It's very important to learn this cast, because it is the basis for many other casting techniques.

Roll Cast

Roll casting isn't a back cast at all. It is a circular motion cast that changes the direction of the line. Instead of being a straight line, roll casts use a tensioned curved loop of line called a "D" loop, but the three casting rules still apply.

Roll casts depend on the back cast forming a smooth, curved loop making the line have minimal contact with the water while the remainder of the loop is perfectly formed in mid-air allowing the power stroke to be delivered with a maximum of efficiency at the instant of water contact. The rod does not stop during a roll cast. It simply changes direction and speed being loaded at all times.

There should be no slack in the loop when the forward cast is made. Simple roll casts can be made with a stationary loop of line drooping to the water's surface from the rod tip. This can be very useful when casting a short distance or straightening the line in preparation for a longer cast.

Longer roll casts are made by forming the loop and delivering the stroke in one continuous motion. The forward cast or power stroke is delivered in an upward direction to insure the line is propelled clear of the water. You should make the cast crisply and aim high.

Single handed roll casts rely directly on fast, snappy wrist action. The "D" loop is formed by elevating the rod to eleven o'clock at a suitable angle away from the body with the arm somewhat extended. The arm is drawn back to the body while the rod is simultaneously swept backwards to two o'clock by the wrist opening up and turning into a loop preparing for the acceleration into the power stroke.

Essentially, what you are doing is moving the rod around slowly and to the back to about two o'clock. Then when the line is below and behind, make the forward cast smoothly stopping at eleven o'clock. Because the line is below and behind, the cast is made upward.

The pear shaped loop made by the tip of the rod is what constructs the "D" loop. By stopping the rearward motion of the line, it allows the leader and the tip of the line to land on the surface to provide the anchor for the power stroke. If the line is not anchored, the energy from the power stroke will be discharged immediately. Instead of the line being propelled forward, the fly will whiplash which could cause danger to you!

An adaptation of this cast is the roll lift. With this cast, the rolling motion is used as a means for lifting a dead line from the water to make a straight line false cast. To do the roll lift correctly, the line must be hit even harder and higher than normal to insure that the line is straight and the fly does not kiss the water when the straight line back cast begins.

The mechanics of each of these methods depends on sufficient energy being applied to a length of line behind the rod to propel it during the forward cast. Every cast is dependent on a good back cast.

Hauling Cast

A haul is a pull or tug on the line that is normally done during the back cast or the forward cast. It increases the speed of the line, enabling you to make longer casts with less strain on your casting arm.

You can also use it during the pickup to ease the line off the water with a shorter stroke than you'd normally need. When a caster hauls during the pickup, he's usually doing it because he is trying to pick up and back cast a long line, one so long that he just doesn't have enough rod travel in his pickup-and-back cast to get the job done.

Before you make your single haul, make sure you have enough slack between your line hand and the reel to permit the longest haul you can make without yanking line off the reel during the haul. To haul on the pickup, begin pulling on the line directly away from your rod hand the instant you begin the pickup.

Your haul should accelerate in time with the rod's acceleration, and it should have its abrupt stop at the same instant as the rod. If you don't need a haul during the pickup, save the line speed you would have used on the pickup for the back cast.

To do this, delay your haul until the line-to-leader connection begins to come off the water. Then accelerate your haul as you accelerate the rod, finishing both the haul and the back cast abruptly at the same instant.

The double haul cast is slightly different than the single haul. With a short, downward pull; draw down about five to eight inches of fly line on the back cast. Bring your hand and the line back up. Let the fly line unroll behind you like in an overhead cast.

Make your second haul in equal length as your first haul. Do this in the acceleration of the forward cast. Bring your hand holding the fly line quickly forward as if you were shooting your line. That completes the cast.

The double haul cast is good for getting you extra distance during your casts.

Reach Cast

In a conventional reach cast, the forward stroke must stop when the rod is high, say at eleven o'clock. And your forward cast must be very slow to give you time to execute the proper reach. The instant after the rod stops, gently reach the rod upstream as the line is falling.

You should finish reaching before the line first touches the water, with the rod pointing perpendicular to the line. In other words, at the finish of a good reach cast, the line does a 90-degree bend at the tip-top of the rod.

To shoot during the reach, completely let go of the line the instant you begin to move the rod upstream. It is imperative that you completely release the line at this point. You'll know you have made a good reach cast when you see the line and leader running dead straight from the rod tip to the fly.

Side Arm Cast

If you're like most people who never tried the sidearm, you'll find it a little weird at first. All the fundamental rod motions are the same— the short stroke and then the gentle acceleration to an abrupt stop. But the muscles doing them are different.

As always, be patient. Get used to the idea that this'll probably feel awkward at first and that you'll screw up a few dozen times before it becomes somewhat familiar.

To make this as easy as possible, you'll want to learn with no more than fifteen feet of fly line (excluding the leader) beyond the tip-top. Because gravity pulls things down, long sidearm casts are very hard to make. With so little clearance to begin with your rod tip travels just about three feet over the ground through both strokes— there's just not time for a long back cast to straighten out behind you before it.

Start with the line on the water or lawn and the rod pointing straight at the yarn or fly. As you make your pickup, do so by bringing the rod up diagonally, off to the side. As you ease into your back cast, make it in a horizontal plane. That's not just "leaned out to the side a little bit", that means that the rod travels perfectly parallel to the ground. Make some false casts in this plane, keeping your casting hand at exactly the same level— no higher — as your elbow.

You'll have best results if you make your hand travel at least eighteen inches during each casting stroke, as though you are making a snow angel with your forearm. If your usual overhead casting style is with your torso square to your target, you'll have an easier time if you turn your torso out toward your rod. To do this comfortably, drop your right foot back and look toward your casting hand as you cast. Otherwise, your shoulder will have to open out a lot on the back cast, which will feel awkward.

A good sidearm cast can be done with your torso upright and comfortable. If you need to make longish sidearm casts, swivel your torso slightly with both the back cast and forward cast, as though you are watching a tennis match from the net. This will give you more line speed, more comfortably than you can generate with a fixed torso. You'll also need to bring the rod up somewhat from horizontal to give the longer line more ground clearance.

False Cast

The false cast can be used for two different operations in fly fishing. First it is used to help in changing directions between casts. It also helps us to set and determine the desistance of the cast to a given point. The false cast is repeated three or four times to help us move to the right or left, not letting it lay on the water until our final cast. Second it is a great cast to use to help dry out a water logged dry fly.

Lift the fly line off the water as in any normal cast. Let the back cast unroll behind you until you feel a slight pull backwards on the rod. Your line should make a small loop.

Bring your fly rod forward but do not let the line settle on the water. Wait until the line is out in front forming a small loop. Repeat all movement until you are ready to make your final cast.

Spey Cast

This cast is good to use in windy conditions. Fly fishing is made possible in many impossible places thanks to this casting technique.

Begin by insuring that the line is straight and tight to the rod. Once you start a spey cast, it's important not to stop the rod until the forward delivery is made. The rod will alter speed and make considerable changes in direction during the cast. Make a slight in-swing up to the ten-thirty position. Rotate your body backwards.

Form a "D" loop behind you with the line the drive the line forward during the turning of your body back towards the front again. The rod is accelerated by pushing with the top hand and pulling with the bottom hand.

The cast should be aimed high and the rod tip must be moved in a straight line if the forward loop is to be kept tight to penetrate the winds. Shooting line to obtain greater distance is important when spey casting. The line is lengthened by releasing spare line immediately after the power stroke is done.

Look for the forward loop of line passing the rod tip. Once you see that, it's time to release, or shoot, the line into the cast. The amount of energy put into the forward cast must be increased to take into account any additional length that is being cast.

General Casting Tips

Take some time to practice before you actually get out into the water. A good idea is to place a target somewhere on the ground in front of you. Then practice landing your fly directly on your target using a variety of casting techniques. This is good for when you are out on the water and want to land your fly where you think the fish are.

Cast your line up river from the location where you think the fish might be. Use a "stop-drop-drop" method of laying your fly on the water. Remember that the idea is to replicate the landing and take-off motion of the fish's natural food – bugs.

When the fly hits the water, loop the fly line over the second and third finger of your rod hand and hold it loosely next to the cork handle. Then take hold of the line with your line hand just in front of the reel so you can strip (pull in) line as needed.

If you're fishing on a river, make one or two up-stream "mends" (rolls) in your line to get the line and leader floating behind your fly. Point your rod tip right at the fly and follow it down the river. Strip in line as needed to keep a straight line between the fly and the rod tip.

When the fish hits, tighten your fingers around the line and the rod handle and raise the rod sharply to set the hook. Keeping your rod tip high let the fish run as the line slides out over your fingers. Palm your reel to slow the fish down and gain control over it, but don't try to completely stop it. Remember to keep your palm flat to avoid being hit by the wind knob.

When the fish rests, reel in quickly. When the fish runs again, palm the reel. Continue this palm/reel cycle until the fish tires and is ready to come in. If the fish runs toward you, stand on your tiptoes, raise your rod as high over your head as possible, and put the line back over the second and third fingers of your rod hand.

Then strip in line as fast as possible to take up slack. If the fish then turns and runs away from you, keep your rod tip high, let the line slowly slide through your fingers, and prepare to palm the reel when all the slack is gone. When landing your fish, keep it in the water and practice proper catch and release techniques.

Of course, the flies you use are an important part of fly fishing as a sport and as recreation. Do you want to know how to tie your own flies? We'll cover that in the next section.

CHAPTER 7: TYING YOUR OWN FLIES

You can buy your flies, if you like, from a sporting goods store, fishing shop, online, or even at Wal-Mart. This is good to begin with, but once you really start getting into fly fishing as a hobby, you are probably going to want to try your hand at tying your own flies eventually.

There are all sorts of books on the market that will teach you how to tie flies. They contain in-depth information for the advanced tier. What we'll do is try to cover just the basics in this section. After all, fly tying is just a small part of fly fishing, although it is important overall.

The first thing you need to know about tying your own flies is to know a little bit about the flies themselves.

Dry flies are simply flies that float. They usually represent adult insects that are emerging (breaking out of their nymphal shuck), drying their wings so they can fly away, or returning to the water to lay eggs.

Since dry flies are the most fun to use (you get to see the fish take the fly), more fly patterns have been designed as dry patterns than any of the rest. Some people separate emerger flies from dries, because they usually float.

Wet flies are simply flies that don't float. They usually represent nymphs and pupae that are swimming toward the surface of the water or trying to break through the surface film to become adults. Since many insects become lunch menu items during this stage of their existence, it's useful to know how to tie wet flies.

Nymphs represent the nymphal or larva stage in an insect's life cycle. Since insects spend most of their life in the nymph or larva stage, this is an important stage in terms of fish forage. I've heard that up to 95 percent of a stream fish's diet is nymphs and larva in some form. Need I say more about the importance of this type of fly?

Streamers are flies that represent minnows, crayfish, leaches and a variety of other life forms that swim under the surface of lakes and streams. Since fish often eat minnows, leaches and crayfish, this is an important type of fly to learn how to tie.

Hooks

You'll need to start your fly tying expedition with a hook. Hooks are what holds the fur, feathers, and any other material you will use to make your fly. If you choose the right hook, your fly will be better proportioned and thus perform better in use. If you choose the wrong hook, you'll have a flawed fly and your success with that fly will likely be less than the success you would enjoy with a properly tied fly.

Let's take a moment to look at the anatomy of a hook. First, the hook has a "gape" or gap. That's the distance between the shank (the part of the hook you tie flies on) and the point. Hook sizes are usually rated by the size of the gape. Second, the hook has a bend.

Depending on the shape of the bend, it will have different qualities and be more suitable to certain types of flies. Third, the hook has an eye. The shape and angle of the eye help determine the possible uses for the hook. Finally, the hook has a shank. As I mentioned earlier, the shank is the length of the hook where the body of the fly is usually tied.

Dry fly hooks come in a variety of shapes and size. Some will have a straight shank and some will have a curved shank. Plus, some are longer than others to accommodate the type of fly you are trying to replicate.

Wet fly hooks are usually heavier than dry fly hooks. Hook bends and shank lengths vary depending on their intended use.

Nymph hooks vary in design more than any other type. Some are designed to tie scuds, others lend their design to stonefly nymphs and some are just good hooks for common nymphs like mayflies and caddis larva. Try to select a nymph hook with a shape similar to the natural nymph you wish to imitate.

Streamers usually imitate minnows, leaches, crayfish or other swimming critters. Their hooks are usually longer than the rest and often have specific bends to accommodate the swimming pattern of the subject being copied. Some hooks are designed for use in poppers for bass and pan fish. These have a hump in the shank to prevent any turning of the popper body.

Fly Vise

When you undertake tying your own flies, the most important tool you'll need is a fly vise. There are many, many choices in fly vises and you might be confused as to which one you will want to buy. Here are a few things to consider:

- The vise should hold a variety of hook sizes and shapes securely. It shouldn't hold just a few either, it should accommodate ALL hooks. If it doesn't, don't buy it.

- The jaws of the vise must be positioned or be able to be positioned at an angle that allows you to tie flies of various sizes with it. Some vises have jaws that are too big to use with a variety of hooks. Others don't have the jaws positioned at an angle that allows the tier to work with small hooks.

- Look for a vise that has jaws positioned at an angle that allows you to work around and with the smallest hooks you might someday use. That might be size 28, so check to see if the vise will hold this size hook securely while allowing complete access to the main length of the hook shank.

- Many vises have heads that pivot or rotate. These are nice features you should consider when shopping for a fly vise. Although a rotary feature isn't a necessity, it is a convenient feature you should consider. Many expert tiers use vises with heads that are fixed and don't pivot or rotate. You'll have to decide if these are important features you're willing to invest in. Keep in mind, a lot of extra features won't make a vise hold a hook any better.

- A good vise should be easy to adjust to fit a variety of hooks. Although many vises will adjust to hold a variety of hook sizes, some are easier to adjust than others. Less adjustment results in saved time and time is money to a commercial tier should you decide to go that route.

- Avoid any vise that takes a lot of time or manipulation to adjust to a specific hook. One or two twists of a knob should be the maximum adjustment required to set any vise to a specific hook. After adjustment, a good vise should clamp down on a hook with a simple twist of a knob, squeeze of a lever or push of a cam. If it's harder than this, let someone less informed monkey with the vise while you tie flies on your new, easy functioning vise.

- The size of the head and jaws of a vise will have an impact on how easy it is to use with certain size hooks. One specific vise on the market has a fast rotary feature that looks nice, but the jaws of the vise are so big it isn't feasible to use with small hooks. Small jaws are easier to work with.

- Another thing you need to consider is how the vise is supported. A clamp is nice if you have a permanent tying bench or you want a vise that just won't move while you're putting pressure on a hook. A pedestal base is convenient if you are working on the kitchen table or traveling. It supports the vise with a heavy base that sets on the table like a lamp would, and it's easy to move. Most vises can be purchased with either a pedestal base or a clamp. Some vises come with both support systems. Try to get a look at both before you buy a vise.

Tools

There really aren't a lot of tools required to undertake fly tying. Here are some basic ones, though, that all fly tyers need.

First is a bobbin to hold your thread. The bobbin will also keep the thread tight while you are tying the fly. Bobbins come in a variety of sizes and shapes, but they all perform the same duty. Good bobbins never cut the thread and cheap bobbins almost always cut the thread, so it's wise to invest in a good bobbin or two.

Good scissors are an absolute necessity for fly tying. This is another tool you don't want to save money on. You'll need at least one pair of scissors to start, but in time you'll want to have several others. All your scissors should have finger loops large enough to fit over your thumb. Anything smaller is just too hard to use.

The first scissor you'll need is one with small, fine points designed to cut thread and fine materials. This should be one designed for fly tying, not something you found at the department store. It can have curved tips or straight ones depending on your desires. The serrated scissors available from Dr. Slick are excellent scissors that will last you many years without trouble. Many other companies offer good scissors too.

Another scissor you'll want to have is a heavy duty one for cutting hair. This can be any scissors designed for that purpose like a heavy fly tying scissor or a heavy hair scissor you might find in a beauty salon or barber shop. Make sure it's stout enough to handle a heavy bunch of hair without working loose at the hinge. I also have an old worn pair of scissors I use to cut wire and other hard materials.

Hackle pliers are small pliers with a constant tension designed to wrap hackle feathers around the hook. They come in all sizes and shapes but all perform the same duty. Some even have a swivel head to make it easy to rotate the hackle around the fly. If you're limited to one set of hackle pliers, select a midge one since it will do all the duties of the larger ones, and it will wrap hackles on flies that are too small for larger hackle pliers.

A bodkin is simply a needle in a handle. You can make your own or buy one at a fly shop. It has many uses including applying head cement, cleaning cement out of hook eyes, picking hair out of fuzzy flies and folding synthetic nymph wings. I'm sure you'll find dozens of other uses, so it's nice to have a couple of these handy tools around when you're tying flies.

Hair stackers are designed to align the tips of hair you're using for wings, heads and tails. They come in a variety of sizes from very small (used on small hair wings and tails) to very large (used on large clumps of hair when spinning hair heads on bass bugs). It's nice to have a variety of these things, but if you can afford only one, get a medium sized one since it will do most of the stacking you need to do.

Now that you have your tools, let's look at tying some specific flies.

Nymph

For this fly, you will need a size 10 to 16 hook, a pheasant tail feather, and black 3/0 or 6/0 thread.

Start the thread on the hook by wrapping it around the shaft a few times securing it with a knot. Then follow these steps to tie your nymph.

1. Pull about 12 strands of feather fiber from a large pheasant tail feather. Since length is important, be sure to get these fibers from the upper 2/3 of the feather. Trim the base of feather stem material.

2. Position the butt ends of the feather fibers about 1/5 of a hook shank back from the hook eye. This leaves room for the head of the fly later. Using two loose wraps, start tying the fibers down to the top of the hook. If you don't start with loose wraps, the fibers will twist around the hook. Once you have the loose wraps in place, you can snug them with downward pressure of the bobbin. This is a rule any time you start tying any material to the hook.

3. Use a slight upward lift on the fibers as you wrap them down to the hook. This will prevent twisting of the fibers and keep them on top of the hook. This is also a rule any time you tie in a tail or any other material that will extend over the bend of the hook. Tie the fibers down to the hook bend adding a couple of extra snug wraps of thread at the hook bend end of the fibers to keep them securely in place and prevent twisting. Wrap the thread back to just behind the hook eye.

4. Start wrapping the fibers forward toward the hook eye. As you get closer to the hook eye, you'll probably need to use your index finger to hold the fibers in place so you can grab them and continue wrapping. Try to adjust your wraps to cover the hook shank yet leave enough fibers to extend to the hook bend or just beyond it.

5. When you reach the place where you started tying the fibers down, tie the fibers off behind the hook eye. Be sure not to crowd the head area just behind the hook eye. This is one problem beginner tyers seem to always have; they crowd the hook eye and don't leave enough room for a proper head on the fly.

6. Tie the fibers down to the hook eye. There should not be any fiber wraps in the head area of the fly, just tied down fibers.

7. Using your thumb and index finger, fold the fibers back toward the hook bend. Grab the fibers with the thumb and index finger of the other hand and pin them to the hook. The fibers should be evenly distributed around the hook, not just on top. Tie the fibers down in the head area of the fly, forming a smooth head. You don't need to make too many thread wraps here, just enough to form a smooth head.

8. Whip finish the head with six to ten wraps of a whip finisher. Since you are tying in the head area of the hook, any whip finisher will do.

9. Cut the thread and cement your wraps with a thin head cement. I've found Griffin Thin head cement to be a good type of cement for this task, but Flexament or any other thin cement will work.

Basic Dry Fly

For this fly, you will need a standard dry fly hook size 10 to 22, 6/0 to 10/0 thread to match the body color, and your choice of fur to match the type of fly you are replicating. Then follow these steps:

1. Start the thread and tie in a tail about the same length as the hook shank.

2. Place a few pieces of the fur you are using on the shank and tie down. A slight upward pressure on the tail fibers while tying them down will minimize the tendency for the fibers to turn around the hook.

3. Wrap the thread around the hook to form the body to approximately 1/3 of the hook shank back from the hook eye. Create a smooth tapered body.

4. Tie in a prepared hackle, curvature (dull side) facing up or forward adding more fur as you go.

5. Using hackle pliers, wrap the hackle forward, dull side facing forward. Keep the wraps even. It doesn't take a killer grip to get the hackle to wrap tightly.

6. When you get to just behind the hook eye, tie the hackle off and trim. If you tied any hackle barbules down over the eye, trim them. You can carefully singe any hackle fibers in the hook eye with a lighter and a hackle guard over the hook eye to prevent singeing the rest of the hackle.

7. Build a smooth head, whip finish and cement.

Once you have the basic idea of fly tying, the rest is just up to your imagination. Experiment around with what you have in your head. Use some trial and error, but most of all, have fun with this new hobby you've learned to add to your other hobby of fly fishing.

So you've got your equipment, you've got your flies, and you're ready to fish. There are some things you should consider when it comes to finding fish to catch.

CHAPTER 8: LEARNING TO FIND WHERE THE FISH

The first step to successful fly fishing isn't fishing at all. It entails taking in your surroundings and observing the area for just a little while. Take fifteen minutes or so to just watch and see if you can observe what the fish are doing.

Look at the bugs that are flying around. Look for evidence of a recent fly hatching that will provide a yummy treat for the trout that are in the water. Where the bugs are is probably where the fish are.

Take a look at grass stems and weeds near the shore line for clues of a recent hatch. Stonefly nymphs crawl out of the water to hatch into adults. This transformation occurs on weeds, grass, rocks and anything else handy near the shore line. Are their cases present anywhere? Mayflies molt after they hatch. This also occurs on grass and weeds. Can you find any clues of a recent mayfly hatch?

While you look for clues of a recent hatch, see if any aquatic insects are crawling around on nearby bushes. Streamside brush is a great hangout for aquatic insects that have recently hatched and are waiting their turn in the egg lying cycle. If you see a lot of a certain kind of insect hanging around the brush, you can bet on patterns that imitate that insect when you get to the stream.

Spider webs are a great place to look for clues. Spiders make a habit of catching insects that fly around their web. If the web is loaded with unfortunate mayflies, the fish are probably loaded with them too. Here's a perfect opportunity to match the size, shape and color of the fly without trying to catch one on the water.

What are the fish doing? Are they rising to flies, and can you see the fly they're eating? If you don't see rising fish, it's not very likely that they'll eat a fly floating on the surface. If you don't see them rising, a nymph might be in order. After all, nymphs are available to them all of the time.

Is there a cloud of caddis flies hovering above streamside brush? Caddis flies are a common sight in the summer hovering above willows and brush. If you see something that looks like a cloud of tiny moths dancing around a streamside willow, grab your box of caddis imitations and start flogging the water with one, you've just solved a mystery.

Fish have three basic needs: food, cover, and a resting place. There are other variations of those, such as fish looking for warmer water in the spring when the water is uncomfortably cold — or cooler water in summer when water temperatures rise.

The first instance puts fish in shallow areas of the stream which the sun has warmed even a few degrees. In the second example the fish move into shaded portions of the stream or to the mouth of a small feeder stream where the water is cooler. Both are examples of the fish seeking comfort.

It will help you immensely in your fly fishing if you start thinking like a fish. If the weather is hot, where do you want to be? You will want to be in a cooler, shady spot? So does the fish.

Fish will generally always face upstream into the current. If the fish were facing downstream, they would eventually end up all the way downstream or in the ocean.

Fish face upstream because that is where their food comes from. Think of it as being in a dining room, and the waitress is bringing you a plate of food — but the food is hanging in the air above the plate.

That is what the fish have, a moving dinner plate. The food comes to them floating on the surface of the water and they have to make the decision to take that food in a split second. Wait too long and it has floated past them. And if the fly you offer doesn't look like the food the fish has been eating? You probably won't get the fish to take your fly.

Also consider the following locations when looking for your fish:

- In riffles and shallows
- In front of boulders where the water speed in front is slowed by the rock behind
- Along the banks where the current is slower and insects fall in the water
- Behind boulders where there is protection from the current
- In drop-offs between riffles
- In protective pockets made naturally by the stream's layout
- In front of surface obstructions where food can get trapped
- Behind logs where there is protection and food in ants
- In back eddies where the current is slower and insects collect
- At the bottom of a deep pool
- In gravel bar shallows late in the evening

- In the shade of an overhanging streamside tree

Remember that where the food is, the fish will be. Fish are opportunists. They will eat whatever is readily available. Fish have to conserve energy. They cannot swim about day and night looking for food. By instinct, they know where the most likely places to find food are.

When you learn what the fish are eating on that particular river or stream, you automatically increase your chances of catching a fish. Get one of those small nets that pet stores use to get small fish out of a tank. Place it on top of the water and see what types of insects you'll get in the net. Match your fly to these insects and you're all set!

One of the greatest joys shared by fly fishermen is the opportunity to visit beautiful places to practice their hobby. Where do you go to find the best fly fishing?

Chapter 9: Recommended Fly Fishing Locations for Your Bucket List

Some people are lucky enough to live close to some great places to fly fish. Others, though, must travel to these places when they want to fly fish. This can be a great travel opportunity and a way to bond over a fishing expedition with fellow fishermen.

Where are the best destinations for fly fishing? Here are a few places recommended along with some highlights of what these destinations have to offer. These are in no particular order.

1. Jackson Hole, Wyoming

Not only is Jackson Hole one of the most beautiful fly fishing destinations in the world, it is home to their very own unique sub-species of trout, known as the Snake River Fine-Spotted Cutthroat trout. These wild and indigenous trout are renowned for their fondness of the dry fly. Jackson Hole is also centrally located in the heart of trout country. Within a two hour driving radius of Jackson Hole is perhaps the most diverse fly fishing region in the world for trout. Opportunities abound, ranging from swift and rugged freestone rivers to glassy spring creeks.

From the vastness of Yellowstone Lake to the intimate alpine lakes of the Wind River Range, still water fisheries are everywhere, providing the solitude not found on the more popular rivers. Easily accessible rivers and lakes are intermingled with remote and rarely fished locations for the adventurous angler. One could easily say that Jackson Hole is the Mecca of fly fishing.

2. <u>Rockport, Texas</u>

Along the Texas coast, there are seven major bay systems that punctuate the coastline. This makes Rockport, Texas one of the most popular salt water fly fishing destinations. These bays are referred to as the Aransas Bay System.

Sea grass carpets much of the shallows in the bay system providing an ideal hiding place for fish as well as acting as an incubator for new fish. It also acts as a filter draining out impurities and making the living environment perfect for fish like speckled trout, red fish, black drum, and flounder.

This area, while warm, is windy most of the year. If you are planning to fish in Rockport, make sure your casting technique is suitable for windy conditions as well as your equipment. Experts suggest an 8 wt. rod with 10-12 # leaders.

There is plenty of water to fish in the Aransas Bay complex. Some of the better known areas that fly fishermen frequent include the Brown and Root Flats (close to the ferry landing near Aransas Pass), the Lighthouse Lakes (just off the Lydia Ann channel), and the backsides of Mustang and St. Joseph Islands. Some of these locations require a boat or kayak to get to; others afford drive-up fishing.

3. Frying Pan River, Colorado

The Frying Pan River is among the best known and loved trout streams in the nation. It is a must for anyone fly fishing in Colorado. The river is located in Basalt, Colorado, which is about a thirty-minute drive from Aspen.

The river is managed to maximize recreation and to grow large, wild trout. Types of Fish: Brook, brown, cutthroat and rainbow, with browns and rainbows most common. Recommended flies are emergers, midges, and dry flies.

Lodging is plentiful for the fly fishing expedition with rustic cabins and hotels dotting the area. This place is well known for fly fishing, so during the busy times, expect to see a lot of other anglers on the river with you.

4. Rapid River, Maine

Some people consider the Rapid River one of the best trout rivers in the United States – even in the world. Fishermen report you can catch brook trout weighing about 5 pounds which is virtually unheard of. Some attribute the size to genetics, while others think it's the amount of smelt fed into the river from nearby Richardson Lake.

This is a short river at 3.2 miles long, but it has some of the best fishing around. You will have to walk about a mile to get to fishable waters, but it's certainly going to be worth it! This is a catch and release river and supports only fly fishing. Species that can be found in the river include brook trout and some salmon.

5. Madison River, Montana

This is a perennial favorite for many experienced anglers. It boasts the highest trout density, the most consistent action, the best dry fly fishing, and the best scenery among its attributes. Located in southwestern Montana, it is also the most fished river growing in popularity every year.

What you will find on the Madison is a straight, clear running pool of water with very few boulders, logs, or tumbling runs. This is a great river for beginners to start with because of its lack of obstacles. The river is easily accessible, easy to wade, and easily drifted.

Species that can be found in the Madison include rainbow trout, brown trout, Yellowstone cutthroat trout, and whitefish. Because this is such a popular destination, lodging and amenities are plentiful.

6. <u>Neah Bay, Washington</u>

Washington is well-known for its amazing salmon fishing. Neah Bay is the perfect place to intercept millions of salmon as they return to rivers from Oregon, Canada, and Washington. The strong currents concentrate the fish as they feed on baitfish and shrimp.

It is possible to catch 10 to 30 fish per day when fly fishing here. Most of the salmon run between 4 and 6 pounds, but every year, there are several reports of salmon weighing in the teens.

It is not uncommon to see fish jump as the bait hits the water, but sink line is recommended.

7. <u>Manistee River, Michigan</u>

This river is a tributary of Lake Michigan and boasts a plentiful supply of trout, steelhead, and salmon. It is a medium sized trout stream in its upper reaches and a large dynamic steelhead and salmon fishery below Tippy Dam. When the trout fishing slows in late fall steel head pick up the pace and vice versa.

The best trout water is found in its upper reaches from the vicinity of Mancelona Road (M-38) downstream over thirty miles to M-66. This stretch of river is small at first (approximately 15-25 feet wide) and gradually gets larger and swifter as it nears the M-66 bridge (approximately 100-120 feet wide).

The upper reaches of this stretch is home to beautiful brook trout. The farther downstream you venture the more brown trout you will find. There is also a healthy population of rainbow trout in the lower reaches of this section. The size of the fish can vary greatly. The overall consensus is that the farther downstream you venture the larger the fish (There are very large trout found in the mid to lower reaches of this section).

The river consists of a sand, silt, and gravel bottom with fallen logs, undercut banks, deep runs, beautiful pools, and sharp bends all creating good holding habitat for trout. In the upper reaches you will find a lot of over-hanging brush and good cover to provide shelter for the trout.

The Manistee River is most famous for its steelhead and salmon fishing. Trout fishing is also excellent and provides anglers with exciting action on both the surface and subsurface for a wide size variety of trout from little brookies to large shouldered brown and rainbow trout. Hatches are prolific stirring the surface with hungry trout during the spring and summer. Streamers and nymphs will produce at almost any time. Steelhead and salmon can be caught on the usual Great Lake fly patterns; egg flies, woolly buggers, wet flies, spey flies, nymphs, etc. If you're looking for an excellent Lake Michigan tributary for exciting steelhead and salmon or for a great trout fishery take a look at the Manistee River.

8. Chattahoochee River, Georgia

Expert fly fishermen say that the tail waters of this famous river have some of the best trout fishing in the deep south. Late autumn and winter are a great time to hit the "Hooch" – as it is commonly known. River flows are more predictable. During this cool period there is less demand for hydropower and with the reservoir low from summer releases, the river flows are less volatile.

The flora and fauna are abundant along the banks of the "Hooch". Conspicuous prehistoric fish weirs (traps) that were originally constructed by Cherokee and Creek Indians out of cobble, and later maintained by white settlers, reveal this area's rich human and natural history. Even an angler doesn't need to catch fish to escape the daily grind of the modern world in this treasure we call the "Hooch".

9. Delaware River, New York

Located in the beautiful Catskill mountains, the Delaware is located in the south central part of New York state and has a rich fly fishing history with a reputation of being one of the best wild trout fisheries in the world. The cold water from the Cannonsville and Pepacton reservoirs, accompanied by the abundance of insects and wild trout, make this river a "must visit" for all fly fishermen.

The greatest reward in fishing the main stem is the opportunity to catch large wild trout. You won't catch enormous quantities of fish in the main stem, but the quality of the fish here is unbelievable. Most fish average from 15 to 18 inches long and weigh between one and two pounds. Fish more than 20 inches long are not uncommon. And these fish are like rocket ships.

Most fish you hook will run you into backing. The chance of fooling one or two of these fish into taking a dry fly is worth its weight in gold.

The biggest problem in fishing the Big "D" is access to the river. Most of the river is public, but the land bordering the river is private, so, fishermen must gain permission from the land owners in order to gain access. Once on the river, you can walk up and down the river because that land is public, up to the river's high-water mark. The river does, however, have some public access points

When fishing this river system, don't get frustrated. There's many a night on this river when fish are rising everywhere and the fishermen can't touch them. This river can humble some of the finest fisherman. These wild fish are well educated and very selective when feeding.

However, when you are fly fishing, you want a challenge, so that is what makes the Delaware so special, and it's what keeps fishermen coming back. Once you've experienced an evening on this river, you will come to appreciate the Delaware trout and look forward to return time and again.

There are, of course, many, many places where you can enjoy fly fishing throughout the world. Alaska, Canada, Belize, and Mexico are all popular destinations and great vacation spots as well!

Just as with any sport, there are certain "rules" that all participants are expected to follow. Fly fishing is no different.

Chapter 10: Fly Fishing Etiquette

The way you are perceived and accepted by fellow anglers may not be high on your list of priorities when learning how to fly fish. However, there are some common courtesy points that all fishermen should abide by to make the experience as pleasant as possible for everyone.

While the rules of politeness may not always be accented in our society as much as it once was, we should have respect for our fellow sportsmen just as they should have the same respect for you.

This also extends beyond treating others with respect, it also entails respecting the resources you are fishing on. The water, the banks, the woods, and all of outdoors should be treated with common courtesy so it is not damaged for future generations. To leave no mark where you have passed in your fishing adventure is showing the ultimate respect.

Here are a few common rules of courtesy you should follow when fly fishing:

1. A section of water belongs to the first person fishing it. It is inconsiderate to crowd an angler who was there first.

2. A slow moving or stationary angler has the right to remain where he/she is. If you are moving, leave the water and quietly walk around the angler in position in the water.

3. If an angler is resting the water, or allowing the water to calm down after some form of disturbance, let them be. Generally, after a fish has been caught, the act of the fight scares the rest of the fish and makes them hesitant to hit on a fly, so you rest the water until it is fishable again. They might be planning their next move too. When an angler is resting the water, it is his or her water. Don't jump in without permission.

4. A person working upstream has the right of way over someone fishing downstream.

5. Always yield to an angler with a fish on the line.

6. Do not enter the water directly in front of someone already in the water.

7. Always recognize property rights. Leave all gates as you found them.

8. Do not litter. If you brought it in, take it out. Leave the area cleaner than you found it.

9. Try not to make tracks whenever possible.

10. Wade only when necessary. The aquatic food chain is fragile.

11. Obey all state and local fishing laws and rules.

12. Never attempt to land someone's fish for them if they have not asked you to help. You do not want the responsibility of losing some guys 'lifetime' fish.

13. Do not offer suggestions on what kind of fly to use unless asked. It is downright amazing what fish will hit on. If you have good luck and a fellow angler isn't, you might say, "This Chicken hole Special really seems to be working, I have an extra if you would like to try it." Mean it, or don't say it.

14. Respect others property rights. That means fences and gates. Close all gates behind you. No trespassing means NO trespassing. You can find out who owns the property and ask permission. Most folks will happily say yes! However, no really means NO.

15. Leave your cell-phone and beeper in the vehicle. There is no place for cell-phones, radios, boom boxes, or worse yet beepers on the river or stream. Your rights are your rights only if they do not infringe on the rights of others. Fishing ought to be an enjoyable experience for all. Don't spoil it for others.

16. Just in case you end up in a situation where some ignorant clod violates any of the "rules" above, explain as politely as possible their error. It sometimes works. Maybe no one ever told them about angling manners.

17. If the clod decides his or her fishing is more important than yours, do not stoop to their level of "clodsmanship". Move on. You probably won't catch anything with the clod (or clodette) there, and the stress of having to be around such people isn't worth it.

People fish to relieve stress, not create it. When you have someone trying to intrude on your peacefulness, it's best just to walk away rather than exacerbate it. Remember that a little common sense goes a very long way when it comes to basic etiquette.

Chapter 11: Conclusion

Fly fishing is an excellent way to explore nature and wildlife and catch a little dinner while you're at it! Many people fish just for the sport of it and release the fish after they catch it. The choice is up to you, but either way, you are likely to find a great deal of enjoyment in this great sport!

As you can tell, there are a lot of components involved in fly fishing, but they are parts that you can easily learn and master with practice. I think you will find that the more you fish, the better you will become just as with any sport.

Of course, there are no hard and fast rules as to what techniques are the best. Play around with your fly rod, see what type of casting works for you, and above all, have fun.

As I said before, fishing can relieve stress, and shouldn't create it. When you relax, enjoy the scenery around you, and have fun, you'll get maximum enjoyment out of your new hobby.

Learn all that you can and always be open to suggestions from other anglers. Just as children learn by watching, we can learn too from watching and listening. Take advice from those who have been there and done that. By that we mean, those who have honed the craft and been met with success.

When you land your first huge fish, the rewards will be well worth the time you've taken to learn fly fishing. Then you can proceed from there and become the type of fisherman you always dreamed of.

Now get out there and look for the fish. When you land a really big one, mount it and hang it proudly in your home. Then you can say, "I caught that one with a dry fly in Colorado". What could be better than that?

MEET THE AUTHOR

Kurt Zeller is an avid fisherman, hunter and general outdoorsman. Kurt lives for the thrill of the hunt or a challenging body of water to fish from on a crisp, cool autumn morning.

Born and raised in Colorado Kurt and his two brothers learned to hunt and fish at an early age and were always allowed on outings with his father, grandfather and many uncles. Kurt still resides in Colorado where he never tires of the Rocky Mountain scenery and some of the best hunting, fishing and camping in the west.

Kurt has used his knowledge and experience of fishing to create Fly Fishing Basics 101. Kurt's goal is to get beginners get started in this popular and fun hobby/sport.

www.ingramcontent.com/pod-product-compliance
Ingram Content Group UK Ltd.
Pitfield, Milton Keynes, MK11 3LW, UK
UKHW022220230426
12048UKWH00016BA/966